YOUR KNOWLEDGE HAS VALUE

AF144620

- We will publish your bachelor's and master's thesis, essays and papers

- Your own eBook and book - sold worldwide in all relevant shops

- Earn money with each sale

Upload your text at www.GRIN.com and publish for free

Daniela Keller

Robert Stalnaker: Common Ground, 2002: A presentation of his paper and an investigation how its theories can be applied to questions.

GRIN Verlag

Bibliografische Information der Deutschen Nationalbibliothek:

Die Deutsche Bibliothek verzeichnet diese Publikation in der Deutschen National-
bibliografie; detaillierte bibliografische Daten sind im Internet über http://dnb.d-
nb.de/ abrufbar.

Dieses Werk sowie alle darin enthaltenen einzelnen Beiträge und Abbildungen
sind urheberrechtlich geschützt. Jede Verwertung, die nicht ausdrücklich vom
Urheberrechtsschutz zugelassen ist, bedarf der vorherigen Zustimmung des Verla-
ges. Das gilt insbesondere für Vervielfältigungen, Bearbeitungen, Übersetzungen,
Mikroverfilmungen, Auswertungen durch Datenbanken und für die Einspeicherung
und Verarbeitung in elektronische Systeme. Alle Rechte, auch die des auszugsweisen
Nachdrucks, der fotomechanischen Wiedergabe (einschließlich Mikrokopie) sowie
der Auswertung durch Datenbanken oder ähnliche Einrichtungen, vorbehalten.

Imprint:

Copyright © 2004 GRIN Verlag GmbH
Druck und Bindung: Books on Demand GmbH, Norderstedt Germany
ISBN: 978-3-638-94205-8

This book at GRIN:

http://www.grin.com/en/e-book/37336/robert-stalnaker-common-ground-2002-a-
presentation-of-his-paper-and

Robert Stalnaker: Common Ground, 2002:

A presentation of his paper and an investigation how its theories can be applied to questions.

1. Introduction

In his paper, *Common Ground,* Stalnaker has the following aim:

> to try to be more explicit about the abstract structure of speaker presupposition
> in order to get clearer about the relations between the presuppositions of different
> participants in a conversation, about the way that what is presupposed changes in
> the course of a conversation (Stalnaker 2002: 701).

Stalnaker defines the terms presupposition, common belief and common ground from a pragmatic perspective and provides counterexamples from a semantic perspective. He constantly compares and defends his theory against other presupposition theorists such as Karttunen, Lewis, Soames, von Fintel and others. When I read Stalnaker's paper for this class, I was very interested in it, because I had a chance to deal with presuppositions in my German school. However, since I never had the time to investigate it in such a deep and controversial discourse, I decided to investigate it further for this course. Stalnaker develops a theory about common ground for declarative sentences. He does not mention questions in his whole paper. As I did the course about questions, I decided to analyze his paper in terms of questions. In this paper, I will first explain Stalnaker's theory for declaratives and then investigate how it can be applied to interrogatives. I will use one wh-question: "Who left?" and one yes-no question: "Did someone leave or not?", and see if there is a change of a presupposition, of common belief or of common ground for the respective question in Stalnakerian theory.

2. Presuppositions

2.1. Different Approaches towards a Definition of a presupposition

There are different ways to define a presupposition according to different theoretical backgrounds. Most common definitions found in dictionaries are standard paradigms and some rough criteria. A paradigm found very often is that "The king of France is wise" presupposes that there is a king of France. "John does not regret voting for Nadar" presupposes that John voted for Nadar. Among the rough criteria which can be found, the most common is the negation criteria, which states that "f sentence S presupposes that ¢, then the negation of S also presupposes that ¢" (Stalnaker 2002: 702). In our example "The king of France is wise" and "The king of France isn't wise" have the same presupposition: "There is a king of France". Other short definitions that can be found are, for instance "the act of presupposing, a supposition made prior to having knowledge" (www.wordreference.com). It often occurs that a presupposition is defined in contrast to an entailment, as in the following case: "presupposition is different from logical entailment because the negation of the proposition does not lead to negation of the presupposed proposition" (Martinovski). Considering all this different kinds of definitions, Kripke said about the phenomenon of presuppositions: "To some degree Justice Stewart's comment about pornography holds here: we all recognize it when we see it even if we can't exactly say what it is." (Kripke 1).

Linguistically, definitions of presuppositions can be divided into semantic and pragmatic definitions. A *semantic* presupposition theory proposes that a presupposition holds between sentence S and proposition Ø if and only if Ø must be true for S to have a truth value. *Pragmatic* presupposition theorists define presuppositions in terms of common ground or speaker presupposition. A proposed pragmatic definition for a presupposition is

Sentence A pragmatically presupposes B if it is felicitous to utter A in order to increment a common ground C only in case B is already entailed by C (Karttunen and Peters 268).

Stalnaker, in this paper, tries a different way of defining phenomena:

> The proposal was that one should describe the phenomena to be explained in terms
> of what speakers tend to take to be common ground when they use certain expressions,
> or what can normally be inferred about the common ground from the use of certain
> expressions, and then try to explain (perhaps in different ways for different cases)
> why the phenomena are as they are. We don't need the mysterious relation X to
> describe the phenomena, and it does not make any contribution to explaining them.
> (Stalnaker 2002: 713).

2.2. Presuppositions and Questions

Further investigation in the analysis of presuppositions in the Stalnakerian definition will be done to see if his definition can also be applied to questions. First, it will be investigated considering the wh-question "Who left?". Alice utters this question. By uttering this question, Alice presupposes that she believes that someone left, otherwise she would ask "Did someone leave?". The question "Who left?" does not inevitably imply that someone left, as it could also be answered by saying "No-one left". But by uttering this question, the speaker presupposes that someone left; otherwise she would not perform this speech act. As Stalnaker defines presupposition in a pragmatic way, in an analysis of **speaker presupposition**, it can be stated that the question "Who left?" presupposes the proposition that someone left, as this is what the speaker presupposes, it is her/his propositional attitude.

After investigating the presupposition of a wh-question, how can Stalnaker's theory be applied to a yes-no question? If a speaker utters the question "Did someone leave?", she/he presupposes only that someone might have left. If we assume that the question is not asked in an ironic way, we can say that the speaker presupposes the possibility that someone left. So the only thing that can be presupposed is that whether someone left or did not leave which cannot be called a presupposition, as Stalnaker states in one of his earlier papers: "This set, which I will call the Context Set, is the set of possible worlds recognized by the speaker to be the "live options" relevant to the conversation. A proposition is presupposed if and only if it is true in all of these possible worlds" Stalnaker 1979: 321f.). By uttering the question "Did someone leave?" in a non-ironic way, the speaker presupposes that it is possible for him that someone could have left. She/he presupposes that it might be true, that it is a possibility for her.

3. Common Belief

3.1. Stalnaker's Definition of Common Belief and how common belief changes with declarative sentences

Stalnaker defines common belief in the following way: "A notion of common belief can be defined for any group of believers in the following way: it is common belief that Ø among a group of believers if all believe that Ø, all believe that all believe that Ø, all believe that all believe that Ø" (Stalnaker 706). This means that Ø can only be common belief if it is believed to be common believed by all participants in the conversation. A declarative sentence can change the common belief. If Alice says to Bob "I can't come to the meeting, I'm going to Balboa Park with my sister" and if Bob speaks English, if he believes that Alice knows whether she has a sister or not and if Bob believes that Alice does not lie to him, then he will believe that Alice has a sister. If we assume that Alice believes that Bob believes that Alice knows whether she has a sister or not, and that Alice believes that Bob believes that she speaks appropriately, then Alice will believe that it is common ground that she has a sister after saying: "I'm going to Balboa Park with my sister". What happened in this conversation was an a*ccommodation* of the proposition that Alice has a sister. Stalnaker states about the phenomenon of accommodation: "The phenomenon of *accommodation*, in general, is the process by which something

becomes common ground in virtue of one party recognizing that the other takes it to be common ground" (Stalnaker 2002: 711).

2.2. Common belief change with questions

If Alice says "Carol left" and if Bob believes that Alice talks appropriately, then Bob will believe that Carol left and there will occur a change of common belief. Whether there is also a change of common belief in a Stalnakerian definition of the term, will be investigated in the following paragraph. By asking "Who left?" Alice shows that she believes that someone left. Bob can believe that someone left, because Alicia would not ask the question if she did not know whether someone left or not. If she were not sure that someone left, she would ask: "Did someone leave?". Still, by asking the question Who left? the answer nobody left is possible. As Alice does not know which person left, she has not seen a person leaving, otherwise she would ask: What was the name of the person "who left?". So it cannot be said for sure that someone left by the utterance, as Alicia has not seen someone leaving. Bob has a less stronger reason to belief that someone left than believing that Alice has a sister when she said: "I am going to Balboa Park with my sister". Whether Bob believes that someone left or not, depends on the situation of the utterance; he might believe it, but it cannot be assumed that he believes it, and so it cannot be assumed that it becomes common belief that someone left just because of Alice asking "Who left?". Alice believes that someone left, but this does not mean that it has to become common believe, but it might become common believe.

What about the yes-no question "did someone leave?"? Does it change the common belief of a conversation? By asking this question, Alice just opens a possibility, she does not claim a proposition. So she cannot change Bob's belief as she does not know what to believe herself. As she does not change Bob's belief she does not change the common belief of the conversation.

4. Common Ground

4.1. Stalnaker's definition of common ground

Stalnaker makes a fundamental distinction between acceptance and belief. His notion of acceptance goes much further than his notion of belief. Acceptance includes belief. Yet belief is just one reason among various others as to why something can come to be accepted. That might be accepted because it is not inherently important for the understanding of the communication. For instance, if Alice says: "The German president, Schroeder, comes to visit the USA", Bob, who knows that Schroeder is not the German president, but the German chancellor, will not deny what Alice said. He understands that the essential proposition of the utterance is "Schroeder comes to visit the USA". Bob might accepted Alice's statement, because he might think that it is not important whether Schroeder is the president or the chancellor or might think it awkward to correct Alicia. Many reasons can be examined to accept something that is not believed. It is possible that only one or some of the participants do not believe what is accepted, but it is also possible that all of them do not believe what is accepted. In a totalitarian regime, people might constantly have to accept to talk about something, as if it were true which they do not believe to be true. Stalnaker defines everything that is accepted in a conversation to be common ground. For his definition of common ground, it is not important, in comparison to common belief, what every participant believes, but what every participant accepts as common ground and believes to be believed by every other participant to be common ground: "It is common ground that Ø in a group if all members *accept* (for the purpose of the conversation) that Ø, and all *believe* that all accept that Ø, and all *believe* that all accept that Ø, etc." (Stalnaker 2002: 716). If the participant's beliefs about the common ground are all correct, Stalnaker talks about a *nondefective* context (Stalnaker 2002: 717).

4.2. Common ground change because of questions

Can the common ground change because of someone asks a question? This should first be investigated for a wh-question. If Alice asks Who left? she presupposes that someone left. Whether Bob believes that someone left or not, he can accept that someone has left, the moment Alicia utters the question. Even though he might believe that nobody left, he could still take it to common ground because he does not want to tell Alice that nobody left for any reason. All the participants in the conversation might take it to be common ground that someone left, when the speaker utters the question Who left?. Bob might answer I don't know and the common ground would go on to be 'that someone left' because of Alice uttering Who left?. All the participants could come to believe that it is common ground among all of them that someone left when Alice asks the question Who left? as long as nobody answers: Nobody left. By the time someone answers Nobody left, a new change of common ground occurs, but this should not be the subject of this investigation. In should be stated now that the common ground can change if the speaker utters the question Who left?.

Yet what about the yes-no question Did someone leave?? Does it change the common ground or not? By uttering this question, Alice only presupposes a possibility, the possibility that someone might have left. So she will not change the common ground by uttering this sentence as there is nothing to be accepted because the speaker does not provide new information which could be brought to be common ground. Some people might think that someone left some will not. But, as long as the speaker does not utter the sentence in an ironic way, there is no proposition that can be taken to be common ground.

5. Conclusion

In this paper I took Stalnaker's *Common Ground* (2002) to investigate his pragmatic theory for questions. I investigated the wh-question who left? and the yes-no question Did someone leave?. For the wh-question, I came to the conclusion that there is a presupposition in the Stalnakerian notion of the term; there might be a belief change and there is a change of common ground. For the yes-no question did someone leave?, there is neither a presupposition included, nor a change of common belief or common ground.

As I struggled with the definition of a 'presupposition' in my school back home, where we learned standard definitions like the negation definition or defining a presupposition in comparison to a definition, I was very interested in learning about a pragmatic definition of the term. It helped me a great deal to get a broader understanding how different approaches to define linguistic terms are applied. When I compare Stalnaker's analysis to what I have learned about presuppositions so far, I wonder if it is still the same thing about which it is talked about. So it should be concluded with the Stalnaker's statement: I suspect that linguists' intuitions about the phenomena of presupposition are intuitions about a number of different things, some more theoretical and some more descriptive (Stalnaker 2002: 713).

Bibliography

Martinovski, Biljana: "Lecture 3: Implicature, Presupposition, Maxims".
www.ling.gu.se/~biljana/st1-97/pragmalect3.html

Nikolis, Georgis: "Praesupposition im Skopus von Einstellungs verben". 02/03/2003.
www.rzuser.uni-heidelberg.de/~gnikolis/presuppositions.pdf

van Rooy, Robert: "A modal analysis of presupposition and modal subordination".
http://turing.wins.uva.nl/~vanrooy/JoS03.pdf

Stalnaker, Robert: "Assertion". in P.Cole (ed.). *Syntax and Semantics 9 – Pragmatics.* New York: Academic Press. pp. 315-332

Stalnaker, Robert: "Common Ground". in: *Linguistics and Philosophy.* 25th volume. Kluwer Academic Publishers: Dortrecht 2002. pp. 701-721

www.wordreference.com/definition/presupposition